CW00458059

A Galw

A Play in One Act

By Geraldine Aron

A SAMUEL FRENCH ACTING EDITION

SAMUEL FRENCH

FOUNDED 1830

New York Hollywood London Toronto

SAMUELFRENCH.COM

ISBN   978-0-573-62204-5   Printed   in   U.S.A.   #9605

A GALWAY GIRL was first staged at The People's Space theatre in Cape Town, South Africa, in October 1979. Keith Grenville directed Ethwyn Grant and Dermod Judge.

For Marion and Helsie.

A GALWAY GIRL

The characters are MAISIE *and* DERMOT. *They begin as a couple in their twenties and age through posture, and voice until they are in their fifties.*

The set is simply two chairs, positioned on either side of a small dining table. The table and chairs stand on a Persian carpet. These items are constant in the lives of the couple. They have been well looked after and are in good condition.

The table should have a tapestry or velvet runner on it with a bottle of whiskey, or a bottle of Guinness and two appropriate glasses: also a few props such as a couple of hard-cover books, an ashtray, hankerchiefs and two pairs of spectacles in cases.

The ideal accents are Galwegian for Maisie and Dublin for Dermot. But any Southern Irish accents will do.

A Galway Girl

DERMOT *is onstage reading a book.* MAISIE *enters with a tea tray. She pours two cups and passes one to* DERMOT. DERMOT *looks at it, slides it back, then pours himself a drink.* MAISIE *disapproves. After a pause, she addresses the audience:*

MAISIE. About an hour after we were married, we were sitting down to our expensive wedding breakfast and Dermot ordered a fry. I thought then I'd made a mistake, but I hoped he was just showing off so I made a joke of it.

DERMOT. (*Taking out & lighting a plain cigarette.*) Maisie was always unusual. Very refined and lovely looking. A shop assistant—but a cut above—even an ejit* could see that.

MAISIE. (*Waving away cigarette smoke.*) After we'd been married a month or so, Dermot stopped going to mass. He just wouldn't get out of bed one Sunday and that was that. He never went again.

DERMOT. (*Livening up & using his arms for emphasis.*) I couldn't take to her family, especially her ould mother. Four-eyes, in the ould grey cardigan, limping around with her rosary beads, giving me leave to call her 'Mammy'. (*He sings to the melody of "Swanee".*) 'Mammy, How I Love Ya, How I Love Ya, My Dear Old Mammy'. Maisie, I said, keep her clear of me—or be Jesus I'll lose me temper. (DERMOT *smokes & reads a book.*)

MAISIE. They say you can tell a lot about a man by the way he treats his mother. Dermot wouldn't have his

---

*idiot, as pronounced in Ireland.

at the wedding—and won't have mine in the house atall atall. Sure that's unnatural going-on, anyone can see that. And Mammy so generous giving us the table. (*She strokes the table, sees a mark & rubs it.*)

DERMOT. Her whole family get on my nerves. A real bunch of know-alls and holy joes. Her sisters think she married beneath her. And didn't the lot of them go to school in their bare feet! Her mother speaks French— for all the good it does her! (*He tosses the book aside, sits lazily, legs spread out.*)

MAISIE. I didn't notice till after, what a rough crowd he went round with. Big coarse-looking fellas in cheap suits. All great talk in a pub—but not at ease in a front room. They're not what I'd in mind I must say—and I dying to be a hostess. Wouldn't you think a man who had his own firm would prefer more *refined* companionship? Well, I won't be mixing with their wives! (MAISIE *develops the posture of a pregnant woman.*)

DERMOT. Maisie went home for her first confinement, so her mother could be in on the act. The ould bitch couldn't wait to phone with the news: "Twas a blue baby, Dermot—sure he never even cried, but I had him baptized, Derm, before he died." (MAISIE'S *pregnancy collapses slowly.*)

MAISIE. I went back to Dublin on the train on my own. But Dermot was there to meet me. (*She looks sadly at* DERMOT.)

DERMOT. Don't be whinging now ducks, you're not the first woman in the world to lose a baby . . . (*He pats her hand across the table. She withdraws the hand.*)

MAISIE. The house was a pigsty—all bottles and butts. He'd had his friends in—spongers the lot of them!

DERMOT. (*Very dramatic.*) Her mother rode in from the West. A vision of holiness in black and grey—her bun bristling with piety. "Musha, Dermot," says she, "Let us kneel in prayer"—and she following me up the stairs: Didn't I swing round by accident and send her flying. Black over grey over black over grey. For a minute I thought we'd lost her. Then the silent heap on the landing stirred and up rose the black and grey Vatican bird!

MAISIE. Godhelpus.

DERMOT. (*Jovial.*) She set her heart on a fur coat. A Persian Lamb if memory serves. But 'twasn't enough to *buy* it—then she had to be *seen* in it! The cocktail bar at The Shelbourne was the venue she had in mind. Ah, she looked great in the ould fur coat. A couple of the boys arrived and we joined them inside for a bite.

MAISIE. (*Bitterly angry.*) I'll never forgive him as long as I live. Oh the pig, the disgusting pig. In the Grill Room at the Shelbourne, with everybody watching, I whispered would he help me into my new fur coat—and the pig dropped it over my head. A gag to amuse his pals. Over my head! May God forgive him.

DERMOT. Our next kid was a girl, and the one after. And then the third one was a girl as well! You'd swear she was doing it to spite me. They were alright when they were babies, but the minute they could back-chat they got on my nerves—the lot of them.

MAISIE. We've moved again, our third house, he never wants to settle down anywhere. But the neighbours here are a better class—especially Mrs. O'Flaherty. She's a great one for fortune telling, but at the same time she doesn't get too familiar.

DERMOT. (*Scornful.*) Maisie's found a friend to her taste. A Mrs. O'Flaherty up the road. A real ould bitch if you want my opinion. Never misses mass and can't have a cup of tea without reading the leaves and making a big production out of it.

MAISIE. (*Worried.*) Dermot's drinking in earnest

now, it makes him snore in his sleep. He shows no interest at all in being a family man—bought a two-seater car, for example. Isn't it a pity they don't make cars with one seat? I can imagine what the neighbours are saying.

DERMOT. (*Incredulous.*) Will I tell you Maisie's idea of heaven? Heaven on earth for Maisie? To go for a spin in the car on a Sunday! When the world is asleep after its Sunday dinner, she wants a family spin.

MAISIE. No interest at all in being a father. He says they're his and he'll feed them and pay their school fees. But that's where he draws the line.

DERMOT. (*Mischievous.*) I'll tell you what we do to oblige Mrs. O'Flaherty: On Sundays the five of us get in the car—a squash but it doesn't matter. Because when we get round the corner I drop them all off. Maisie and the kids go to Mass and where I go is my own affair.

MAISIE. (*Furious.*) The disgrace of Dermot, drinking on a Sunday, when he knows it upsets me so much. One week I walked past the pub—to see was it crowded. An ejit playing an accordian. Children eating crisps in the gutter, and himself in, treating the scroungers.

DERMOT. (*Fed up.*) I can see now that I'd have been better off with a common one. Her ladyship wants me to eat salad cream. Amn't I easy enough to please when a fry will do me every night? But no. Nothing will do her but private schools and salad cream.

MAISIE. (*Primly.*) I'm not saying Dermot is common, sure that would reflect on myself. Didn't I choose him when I had many a choice? But all the same there's oddness in a man who'd rather starve than eat anything different. Fry, fry—every night a fry!

DERMOT. (*Slowly, weighing his words.*) I'm not a man who likes to get rough, but in certain situations I can see why it's necessary. Such as Maisie dictating to me what I'll eat. And making a mockery of me in front of the kids.

MAISIE. (*Tight-lipped.*) My family was right when they said he was beneath me, and when my mother said he'd a vicious streak she must have been having one of her premonitions. Dermot hit me this morning, for no reason at all. And when one of the kids screamed, didn't he hit her too, the bully. (*She turns her back on* DERMOT.)

DERMOT. (*Frustrated.*) Maisie moved into the spare room. I can imagine who put her up to it. I'm not a great philosopher but this I'll tell you: The curse of the Irish is their mothers. (MAISIE *folds her arms on the table & rests her head, looking downstage.*)

MAISIE. (*Very soft & wistful.*) Lying there on my own, with himself snoring in the next room, I realized I'd missed the boat entirely. Wasn't I a fool to be taken in by his sweet talk? But wasn't I twenty-six, and hadn't nobody else proposed to me! It's just that marriage isn't at all how I thought 'twould be. I'd visions of the two of us going to the pictures, drinking Ovaltine in front of the fire, and, on a wet Sunday, the kids and their Dad playing Snap in the attic. Sure wasn't I a country girl when all's said and done. An innocent young one from Galway. (*She sits up.*) Snap in the attic my eye!

DERMOT. (*Cocky.*) She's still hiding out up above, but I've a plan of my own. The boys'll be round for a couple of jars—and we'll soon see who's boss when I order the sandwiches!

MAISIE. (*Furious.*) Dermot brought half the pub home—singing in Irish—the great patriots. I had to come down in my dressing gown to make them their sandwiches. The big, common clods—with their oily heads!

DERMOT. I married Maisie for her modesty, but I didn't think 'twould go on forever! You can't get as much as a kiss out of her until the curtains are closed—and we living at the top of a hill! Maybe, says she, there'll be a helicopter passing. You'd need the patience of a saint, I'm telling you.

MAISIE. There isn't an opera Dermot can't sing, or a book he hasn't read. He could recite whatever you like, backwards, without taking a breath. So isn't it a wonder he has such peculiar ideas? According to him, the Pope's a waste of time, Shakespeare was a Dublin man, and Princess Margaret is Jewish.

MAISIE. (*Reluctant to speak.*) Some things are better not told, for fear some fool would decide to imitate them—resulting in *twice* the unhappiness. But, between ourselves, Dermot went too far last night. He followed me into the children's room, picked up their potty from under the bed, and—NO! Some things are better left unsaid.

DERMOT. (*Orating.*) When is a hat a potty? *WHEN IT'S UNDERNEATH A BED.* And when is a potty a hat? WHEN IT'S ON A MOTHER'S HEAD!

MAISIE. God forgive him.

DERMOT. (*Excited.*) What did I tell you about that O'Flaherty one? What did I tell you? Didn't the rip call the police when I raised my voice in the privacy of my own home. If she sets foot in this house again I won't be responsible.

MAISIE. (*Very distressed.*) The disgrace. The disgrace of it. The whole street up with its ears cocked. The children screaming, and the Garda arriving in the van. They pushed Dermot down the stairs ahead of them. Head over heels over head over heels. He didn't stir for a second or two and I wondered would I mind if he was dead. Next thing he was up, bawling and kicking. Bastards, says he, and the kids listening. Oh the disgrace of it, the disgrace.

DERMOT. (*Cheerful.*) Met a grand fella at the station last night. In for drunken driving—and a baby Powers*

*If not understood, substitute 'an emergency bottle'

in his sock! Sure, we'd a great time, talking our heads off. Dermot, says he, isn't the Catholic faith a wonderful institution the way it stops our wives abandoning us? We'd a good laugh over that and I told him what Maisie said when the Garda manhandled me: "Careful, careful, he's not a well man" I'll tell you something, I'm still her ould fella—for all her airs and graces!

MAISIE. (*Putting on her spectacles.*) I pity him, in spite of myself, running around, buying friends. Sure, popularity's something you're born with, he'll never see that. Finoula, our middle one's a lot like him. Stubborn as a mule with ideas of her own. A dreamer if ever there was one. Oona, the eldest, is like a closed book—never gets herself too excited. The house could be on fire, Dermot could be murdering me and Oona would be found with her nose in Treasure Island. Ailish, the youngest, seems a straightforward child.

DERMOT. Maisie's always going on about family outings, nagging away like a squeaking chalk. So I said I'd take Finoula to the Air Show. Now I'm sorry to say this about my own flesh and blood, but the kid hasn't an iota of personality. Silent as a tomb on the journey out. Giving me sly looks every two minutes, didn't want sweets or icecreams and wouldn't go on the bus-helicopter after I'd laid out a pound. Not an experience I'd care to repeat.

MAISIE. Have you ever heard of a man who'll admit that he doesn't like his own children? The kids next door are better looking, the kids up the road are more intelligent, the kids down the lane are better company, the kids round the corner can take a joke. Is it any wonder his own keep from getting under his feet?

DERMOT. Let me make this perfect clear: Boarding school was as much her idea as mine. The same plan for different reasons.

MAISIE. 'twill give them the stability a child needs.

DERMOT. 'twill give me the independence a man needs. So off they went, with their three long faces. Isn't it a wonder a character like me would get kids like them? Sure that's genes gone daft entirely.

MAISIE. Dermot went to London on a holiday, and stayed so long I thought I was separated. Then one night he phoned—a trunk call from England, begging me would I come over:

DERMOT. I was wondering—

MAISIE. says he

DERMOT. would you like to come over and see a few sights?

MAISIE. I might—

DERMOT. says she

MAISIE. and I mightn't. How do I know I'll be welcome?

DERMOT. (*Getting irritable.*) Amn't I ringing up to invite you?

MAISIE. says he

DERMOT. Take it or leave it. I've got to go. Are you coming or aren't you?

MAISIE. (*Hastily.*) I am, so.

DERMOT. (*Tender & affectionate.*) The face on Maisie when she saw London! The big, round eyes of her. She's always dressed well by instinct, and to see her strolling in Bond Street you'd never say she was a Galway girl—She could have been anybody! We linked our arms and had our photo taken.

MAISIE. (*Shyly.*) At my age I thought it was the change beginning, but then I got definite signs. His nibs is delighted, though I'm sad to say it'll be a five minute wonder like the other three were. But you never know— a person can always count on Dermot to be unpredictable.

DERMOT. (*Delighted.*) He's a little fella! With a big, red face—blond hair and a bawling mouth! The image of meself! The bloody image! If you could hear the ejit's names she wanted to call him. I put my foot down and had my say—Ted is his name and Ted's what he'll stay.

MAISIE. (*Picking up a handkerchief.*) He was never like this over the others—let's hope it lasts. I won't say he feeds him, or baths him or anything. But I've seen him looking into the cot with a silly expression on his face, Godhelpus. (*She dabs at her eyes, blows her nose.*)

DERMOT. (*Frightened.*) All of a sudden, after being my own boss for donkey's years, everything's gone rotten. Wasn't I making the best electric fire elements in Ireland? And didn't a German bastard set up in competition? And wouldn't I be as well off—or better—on a salary in London? She'll have to forget about ponies and private schools. Let the brats go and find themselves jobs. (DERMOT *puts his spectacles on & reads his book.*)

MAISIE. The disgrace of living in London, in a place like this. Not fit for a family of one—let alone six. The landlord goes round in a grey-looking vest, I'm ashamed to wheel Ted in his pram. And the girls are in jobs and they still children. Oh Jesus, Mary and Joseph hear my prayer. *God* hear my prayer. (If there *is* a God.) (*She crosses herself.*) May God forgive me.

DERMOT. (*Ruminating.*) You grow up automatically disliking the English, but you only find out why you hate them when you have to live among them. They haven't our sense of humour, and they think all the wrong things are important:

MAISIE. (*Breathless with annoyance.*) I'll never hold my head up again, we're the laughing stock of the street! Dermot called in Meals-on-Wheels to embarrass me. And the social worker, a young one with big brown eyes straight from the bible—wouldn't believe 'twas a joke.

DERMOT. (*Glasses off for the moment, slightly drunk.*) Now I may not be a philosopher but I can tell you this: The poetry in a man's soul is more important than the size of his bank balance: Isn't it true? Better the bird in flight than the dead turkey. The laughter in a man's heart is worth twice as much as the food in his stomach. Better the bird in flight—sure I've already said that—you bunch of goms!

MAISIE. If we had money they'd say he was eccentric. But when you're hard up they call it unbalanced. The landlord gave us notice and Dermot says it's up to the State to see that we're housed.

DERMOT. (*Self-righteous.*) I've been paying them tax all my life!

MAISIE. says he—and we only in England six months. When I think of my childhood in the country. The big wardrobes. The family at mass with Mammy and Daddy. My four brothers with their thick hair and suntanned legs. Like the Kennedys. And here I am in last year's coat, amongst common people and I always so refined. Dermot gone off and not a word, not a care for his family, not even for Ted.

DERMOT. (*Smiling a bit foolishly.*) Rough patch. Rough patch. A drop of John Jameson on the brain! Of course Maisie was always reliable—she managed to find us a place. Nothing you'd want to take snaps of, but adequate till I recover my health. Oona's gone to America. Finoula's gone to Australia. Ailish has gone to The Hebrides. Just my wife and my boy and myself—and a bit of peace and prosperity, DV. (*He replaces his spectacles & wears a peaceful expression.*)

MAISIE. I'm not saying he's suddenly become the ideal husband, a devoted Catholic or the perfect father. But things are more peaceful with the girls gone. Frankly though, they could have made their point without going so far. Australia, America, The Hebrides, my eye!

Wouldn't elsewhere in London have had the same effect? I can imagine what the neighbours are saying. (*She shuffles her shoulders, in a huff.*)

DERMOT. I'm a sick man alright, more or less stuck in my room for the moment. 'Emphysema' says the quack in his ould English accent. Caused by years of smoking sixty a day. It can gallop or creep, says he, the rate of progress is up to you—smoking is out of the question. Maisie, says I, and he still at the door, bring an ashtray and matches in here please. (*He chuckles but loses his breath & coughs.*)

MAISIE. (*Dreamily, far away.*) Ted was killed in a road accident. He went through the door with his big, innocent face smiling goodbye. And never came back, the lamb. Dermot hasn't moved from his room. Isn't it desperately sad, and Ted his favourite.

DERMOT. (*Briskly changing the subject.*) My daughters married husbands just like themselves—dull fellas, lacking in personality. Finoula was home for Ted's funeral. I did my best to get a rise out of her husband, but sure nothing would budge that type. Smug as a bug in a bloody ould rug.

MAISIE. (*Still far away.*) The excitement is over. No more visitors, phone calls, or letters of condolence. Finoula went home looking older than thirty. She was very fond of Ted, Godhelpus.

DERMOT. (*Huffy & nervous.*) They'll hospitalize me over my dead body! If a person is sick the last thing he wants is a bunch of Jamaicans experimenting on him. I'll stay where I am, in my own home. And if my children can't bother to write to me—even a card—that's their concern.

MAISIE. (*Much older & wiser.*) Just myself and himself again, and two television sets. Our usual meal is a fry. Our favourite drink is tea. There's isn't much left to argue about. When there's something good on the

telly I give him a signal for fear he'd miss it, watching
the wrong channel: I tap on the wall with the head of
the tongs: (*She taps once.*) One tap for BBC 1 (*Taps
twice.*) Two taps for BBC 2 (*Taps three times.*) Three
taps for ITV. Of course they'd have to be landing on the
moon before *he'd* signal *me*. But that's Dermot for you.
Though an odd time he'll call me in when he feels like
an audience.

DERMOT. (*Removing his spectacles & looking youth-
ful.*) Are you listening? Three of us—I suppose we were
seventeen or so—hi-jacked a bus from the terminus: We
chose a route and off we went—real divils! When the
passengers got on at the bus-stops, we asked their
destination and told them the fare: A gumdrop missus,
or two eggs, a Mars Bar as far as Ball's Bridge. I've
never had such gas! We took everyone right to their
doorstep—they thought it was bloody Christmas. "Sure
it's the new tramways policy to be more obliging Missus"
says I to an ould one. I've never had such gas. (*Dis-
tantly.*)

MAISIE. One evening late, when our TV's were off I
heard Dermot singing to himself.

DERMOT. (*Standing and singing.*) "Darling, you are
growing O-Old. Silver threads among the gold . . ."
(MAISIE *listens, then stands up & looks at* DERMOT.)

MAISIE. I went in and we looked at each other, the
first time we'd looked in years.

DERMOT. (*Embarrassed.*) What are you gawpin' at—

MAISIE. says he—

DERMOT. —amn't I singing to my reflection in the
wardrobe mirror!

MAISIE. (*Pleased with herself.*) Are you, so?

DERMOT. says she—

MAISIE. and your hair as stubborn a *red as it ever
was! (*They sit down again.*)

---
*brown/black

(DERMOT *puts his spectacles on, fumbling slightly.*)

DERMOT. I'd rather die than write to any of those brats. Bad cess to them—they'll be sorry when it's too late. Sure I've more brains in my little finger, than their three husbands knocked together. Bad cess to the lot of them!

MAISIE. Like it or not he was taken to hospital, oxygen tent and all. At visiting time he whispered to me—

DERMOT. (*Whispering.*) Will you loosen the sheets at the end of the bed before my feet go gangrene.

MAISIE. But the nurse said no, the sheets must stay tucked in, in the interests of neatness and hygiene.

DERMOT. (*Leaning back weakly but trying to be perky.*) This is the place where his nibs Douglas Bader had his wooden legs screwed on. He has his plaque stuck up in the entrance hall. Sure the English make heroes out of people on the slightest excuse. Didn't many a fella lose his legs in shunting accidents, for example, and not a word about it? But you'd die laughing in this place. All day long the inmates tell stories about their wives. But when visiting time comes, there they are, holding hands, kissing each other and talking rubbish in whispers. (*He folds his arms but they slowly uncurl.*)

MAISIE. I was always relieved when the bell rang, because to tell you the truth, Dermot and I found it difficult to chat for an hour. He was very weak the last time, too weak to start an argument even. And when the bell rang and I stood up (*She stands up.*) he kept his eyes closed and tapped his cheek with his finger. (DERMOT, *eyes closed, taps his cheek with his index finger.*) At first I thought he was telling me something about shaving, or toothache, (*She goes to* DERMOT'S *side of the table.*) But he went on tapping till I leaned down and kissed the spot. (*She slowly bends to kiss his cheek.*) (DERMOT *nods once then remains perfectly still.*) And that was the last I saw of him.

(DERMOT *is not seen to die, but his passing is indicated by a fading light on him.*)

MAISIE *walks a few steps downstage. She removes her spectacles, speaks calmly & without sentiment.*

MAISIE. I'd feel like a stranger in Ireland now, so I may as well stay where I am. Without Dermot to say I'm putting on, I get on well with the English—and have many a visitor in. I spend holidays with my daughters whenever I like, and their husbands are welcome here. The house is as clean as a new pin with never the smell of a fry.

She returns to her chair and sits much as she did at the beginning. DERMOT *is now in shadow.* Yet sometimes, when there's something worthwhile on television I find myself knocking with the head of the tongs: One tap for BBC 1 (*She taps once, quite lightly.*) Two taps for BBC 2 (*She taps twice, still briskly.*) Three taps for ITV. (*She taps three times, very slowly.*) (MAISIE *smiles and the lights fade to blackout.*)

THE END.

PRODUCTIONS

A GALWAY GIRL was produced at The Space Theatre
  in Cape Town, South Africa in 1979.
The Druid Theatre, Galway, Ireland in 1979
The Edinburgh Festival, Scotland 1980
The Lyric Theatre, London 1980

PROPERTY PLOT

Small dining table with velvet or tapestry runner on it.
2 dining chairs
Cupboard or sideboard containing bottle of Guinness or
    whiskey, a glass and a bottle opener.
2 hardcover books without dustjackets.
A persian carpet to be placed under the table.
ON TABLE: Cigarettes, matches, ashtray, reading
    glasses in cases.
Tray with two cups, saucers and spoons, teapot, sugar
    bowl, milk jug. (MAISIE)
Handkerchief (MAISIE)

Both MAISIE and DERMOT should be inconspicuously dressed, bearing in mind that the play spans thirty-five years. A print dress for MAISIE and a dark suit for DERMOT have proved acceptable.

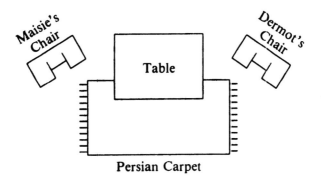

Sideboard or cupboard

Maisie's Chair

Dermot's Chair

Table

Persian Carpet

A Galway Girl

FLOOR PLAN